WHAT IF YOU HAD

T. rex Teeth!?
And Other Dinosaur Parts

by Sandra Markle

Illustrated by
Howard McWilliam

Scholastic Inc.

For Sara Adkins
and the children
of Magness Creek
Elementary
School in Cabot,
Arkansas

The author would like to thank the following people for sharing their enthusiasm and expertise: Dr. David Button, North Carolina State University and North Carolina Museum of Natural Sciences, Raleigh, North Carolina (*Brachiosaurus*); Dr. Kenneth Carpenter, Museum Director, USU Eastern Prehistoric Museum, Price, Utah (*Ankylosaurus*); Dr. Greg Erickson, Florida State University, Tallahassee, Florida (*Tyrannosaurus rex*); Dr. Andrew Farke, Raymond M. Alf Museum of Paleontology, Claremont, California (*Stegosaurus* and *Triceratops*); Dr. Denver W. Fowler, Dickinson Museum Center, Dickinson, North Dakota (*Velociraptor*); Dr. Stephan Lautenschlager, University of Birmingham, Birmingham, United Kingdom (*Therizinosaurus*); Dr. Jordan Mallon, Canadian Museum of Nature, Ottawa, Ontario, Canada (*Edmontosaurus* and identification of dinosaur scientific names for timeline); Dr. Adam Marsh, Petrified Forest National Park, Holbrook, Arizona (*Dilophosaurus*); Dr. John Scannella, Dr. John R. Horner, Curator of Paleontology, Museum of the Rockies, Bozeman, Montana (*Triceratops*); Dr. Paul Sereno, University of Chicago, Chicago, Illinois (*Spinosaurus*); Dr. Tom Williamson, New Mexico Museum of Natural History, Albuquerque, New Mexico (*Parasaurolophus*).
A special thank-you to Skip Jeffery for his loving support during the creative process.

Photos ©: cover inset: sruilk/Shutterstock; back cover top: Linda Bucklin/Shutterstock; 4: Science Photo Library/Mark Garlick/Getty Images; 4 inset: Phil Degginger/age fotostock; 6: Warpaint/Shutterstock; 6 inset: Dinoton/Shutterstock; 6 background: Herschel Hoffmeyer/Shutterstock; 8: Leonello Calvetti/Getty Images; 8 inset: Justin Tallis/Getty Images; 8 background: Herschel Hoffmeyer/Shutterstock; 10: CoreyFord/iStockphoto; 10 inset: Francois Gohier/ardea.com/age fotostock; 12: Warpaint/Shutterstock; 12 inset: Andy Crawford/Dorling Kindersley/Getty Images; 12 background: Herschel Hoffmeyer/Shutterstock; 14: Elenarts/Shutterstock; 14 inset: Evgeniy Mahnyov/Alamy Stock Photo; 16: José Antonio Peñas/Science Source; 16 inset: Millard H. Sharp/Science Source; 18: Warpaint/Shutterstock; 18 inset: Ken Lucas/Getty Images; 18 background: Herschel Hoffmeyer/Shutterstock; 20: Stocktrek Images/Getty Images; 20 inset: Oleksiy Maksymenko/age fotostock; 22: Catmando/Shutterstock; 22 inset: Mohamad Haghani/Alamy Stock Photo; 22 background: Herschel Hoffmeyer/Shutterstock; 24: XiaImages/Getty Images; 24 inset: dpa picture alliance/Alamy Stock Photo; 24 background: Linda Bucklin/Shutterstock; 30 left: Ben Molyneux/Alamy Stock Photo; 30 right: Gehrke/Shutterstock.

What if one day when you woke up, you felt a little bit strange? Then you discovered one part of your body was now VERY different! What if, overnight, a dinosaur's body part had taken its place?

TYRANNOSAURUS REX

(tie-RAN-oh-sawr-us rex)

Tyrannosaurus rex was a meat-eating dinosaur with a mouthful of around 60 seven-inch-long teeth. Its teeth were thick and slightly curved. Plus, each tooth had sharp, jagged edges like a steak knife. When a *T. rex* closed its jaws, its upper and lower teeth locked like fingers lacing together. Scientists also believe this dino's jaw muscles slammed its mouth shut with bone-busting force. That's probably why scientists have found bones from other dinosaurs with *T. rex* bite marks!

FACT

T. rex broke and lost teeth when it bit into bones, but fossils (preserved remains) of its jawbones show that this dino was always developing replacement teeth.

If you had a *Tyrannosaurus rex's* teeth, you'd never need a knife to cut up your food.

VELOCIRAPTOR

(veh-LOSS-ih-RAP-tor)

A *Velociraptor*'s sickle-tipped toes—the second toe on each hind foot—were just what this meat-eating dinosaur needed to grab dinner. A *Velociraptor* was rather small—probably only six to seven feet long from its nose to the tip of its tail. Its skeleton shows it ran like a bird on short hind legs with big feet, holding its sharp toes off the ground. Scientists think this dino sneaked close to its prey, leaped, and put those sickle-tipped toes to work. Then dinner was served!

FACT

A *Velociraptor* had perfect meat-eater teeth—pointy and sharp-tipped, with a steak knife–like jagged inner edge.

If you had a *Velociraptor*'s sickle-tipped toes, you could open presents in a flash.

STEGOSAURUS

(STEG-uh-SAWR-us)

A *Stegosaurus* was a giant plant-eater with a built-in defense—a spiked tail. Each side of its tail tip had a pair of nearly two-foot-long spikes! Because a *Stegosaurus*'s tail was made up of around 45 to 49 different tailbones, scientists think it could easily swing its tail side to side, and maybe even up and down. WHAM! A spiked-tail slap was sure to back off an enemy.

FACT

A *Stegosaurus* had thin, flat plates sticking out of its back. Scientists believe they were most likely to show off and win a mate.

If you had a *Stegosaurus's* spiked tail, you'd always be ready to toast marshmallows by the campfire.

PARASAUROLOPHUS

(par-ah-SAWR-OL-uh-fus)

Parasaurolophus had an amazingly long crest on top of its head—some crests were as long as five feet! X-rays and CT scans of fossil skulls have shown scientists this crest was full of the dinosaur's breathing tubes. These tubes stretched to the end of the crest and back again before going down its throat. Scientists tried blowing air through model crests to figure out what this dino might have sounded like. They learned that the length of the crest affected the sound it made, giving each *Parasaurolophus* its own voice.

FACT

Scientists believe the size and shape of *Parasaurolophus*'s ear bones mean that this dino was best at hearing deep sounds that carried over long distances.

If you had a *Parasaurolophus's* head crest, you could lead the school marching band.

ANKYLOSAURUS

(ang-KILE-uh-SAWR-us)

Ankylosaurus was a tank of a dinosaur with a full coat of body armor. That armor was made up of rows of bone plates within its skin. Scientists have discovered many similar kinds of dinosaurs, which they have grouped together as ankylosaurs. Some of these dinos had flat bone plates for their armor. Others had plates with spines or spikes. At least one kind of ankylosaur even had armored eyelids! But all of them topped off their protective armor with a bony, helmet-like skull.

FACT

Some kinds of *Ankylosaurus* had a built-in weapon—a stiff tail tipped with a club made of three or four fused armor plates.

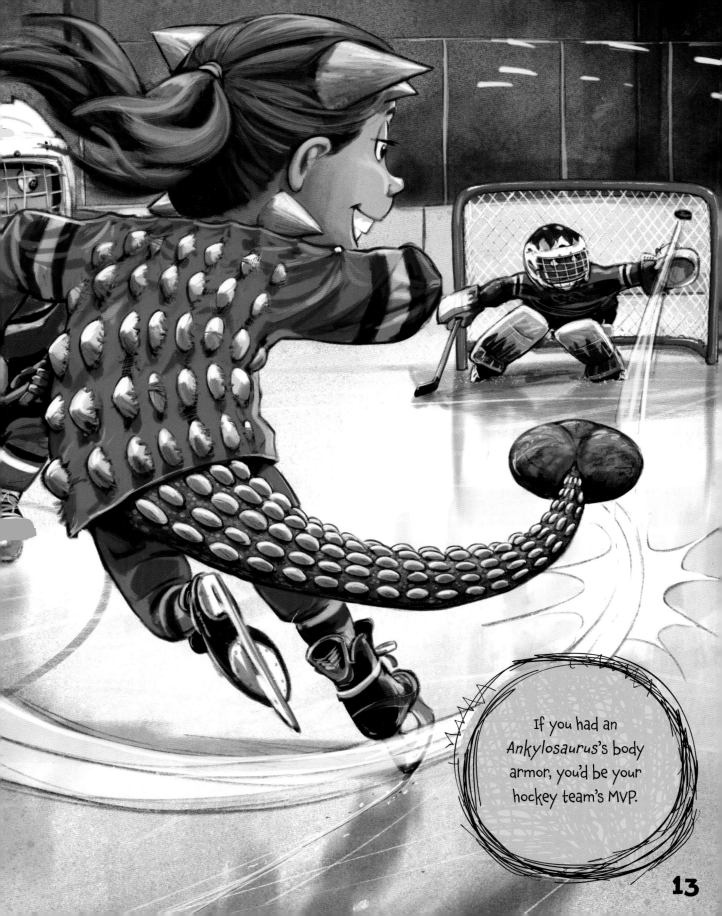

If you had an
Ankylosaurus's body
armor, you'd be your
hockey team's MVP.

BRACHIOSAURUS

(BRACK-ee-uh-SAWR-us)

Brachiosaurus was a plant-eater with a long neck perfect for munching treetops. Its neck was nearly 30 feet long, which let it reach as high as a three-story building! This dino's 13 huge neck bones were full of holes so that its long neck was light enough to lift. Since its teeth weren't very good for chewing, its gut had to do all the digesting once it swallowed. And what a long swallow it had!

FACT

This dinosaur was named *Brachiosaurus* because its front legs are longer than its back legs—*Brachiosaurus* means "arm reptile" in Greek!

If you had a *Brachiosaurus's* neck, you could easily see over everyone's heads at the movies.

THERIZINOSAURUS

(thair-uh-ZEEN-uh-SAWR-us)

Therizinosaurus had front limbs that were tipped with nearly two-foot-long claws. At first, scientists thought those long claws meant this dinosaur was a hunter. But after studying fossils, scientists learned *Therizinosaurus*'s claws were thin—probably not good for catching prey. Plus, this dino had a plant-eater's beak and only teeny-tiny teeth. Now scientists believe *Therizinosaurus* was a plant-eater that used its giant claws to bring leafy branches close enough to grab a mouthful.

FACT

Because *Therizinosaurus* had such small teeth, scientists believe it also swallowed stones to help its belly smash up every leafy mouthful.

If you had a
Therizinosaurus's
claws, you would
make the best hedge
sculptures.

EDMONTOSAURUS

(ed-MON-tuh-SAWR-us)

Edmontosaurus's shovel-shaped jaws made its mouth perfect for scooping up shrubby plants. As its jaw muscles pulled its mouth closed, the hard beak at the front snipped off each bite. Next, muscles moved this dinosaur's big jaws to crush its food between bunches of small teeth—almost 700 total—packed so close together they acted like giant molars. Scientists believe this dino wasn't picky and ate whatever it could scoop up—leaves, berries, seeds, and even little shellfish.

FACT

Rare rocks that formed from mud where an *Edmontosaurus* once lay show that its body was covered with small six-sided scales.

If you had an *Edmontosaurus's* shovel-shaped jaws, you would win every food-eating contest.

19

TRICERATOPS

(tri-SERRA-tops)

Triceratops's giant skull was armed with three horns. An adult's nose horn was about a foot long. But the two brow horns—one above each eye—poked out about three feet! Behind those horns, its head and neck were shielded by a helmet-like "frill." Scientists think being armed and armored let this dino put up a good fight if a meat-eater attacked. But scratches found on *Triceratops* horns may also mean these dinosaurs clashed horns in battles for mates.

FACT

A *Triceratops*'s brow horns showed its age. Babies had nubs, teenagers had horns that curved up, and adults had very long horns that aimed forward.

If you had a *Triceratops*'s horns, you could carry all of the groceries in one trip.

DILOPHOSAURUS

(dye-LO-fuh-SAWR-us)

Dilophosaurus was an eight-foot-tall dino with long hind legs. Scientists studying its skeleton have found lots of places where big muscles attached to its hind legs. This is proof this dino was fast! Its footprints also show that Dilophosaurus stepped on just three toes and a footpad. So it was probably light enough on its feet to make quick turns and big leaps. Since it had sharp meat-eater teeth, Dilophosaurus probably chased down fast food.

FACT

Scientists think Dilophosaurus's bony head crests helped this dinosaur spot more of its kind.

If you had a
Dilophosaurus's hind
legs, you would be a
star dancer.

SPINOSAURUS

(SPY-nuh-SAWR-us)

Spinosaurus had a giant sail on its back. This was made up of skin coated with keratin (the same tough stuff human fingernails are made of) and held up by six-foot-long spines. This dino's skeleton shows its backbones were locked together. Scientists believe that kept its sail upright and always fully spread open. All the better to show off! The giant sail was sure to catch a future mate's eye, and it—maybe—made *Spinosaurus* look too big for other dinosaurs to attack.

FACT

Spinosaurus's broad back feet, long toes, and flattened toe claws probably kept it from sinking into the mud while hunting for a shallow-water meal.

If you had a *Spinosaurus*'s sail, you'd be a champion windsurfer.

Dinosaur parts could be cool for a while. But you don't need a 30-foot-long neck to reach your food or a super-strong bite to eat it. Your voice sounds just fine without a long head crest to fine-tune it. And you don't need a giant

sail to be noticed. But if you could keep any dinosaur part for more than a day, what kind would be right for you?

Luckily, you don't have to choose. You aren't living long ago in the Age of Dinosaurs—you're living now! All of your parts are people parts.

They are exactly what you need to be the one and only you.

WHAT MADE A DINOSAUR A DINOSAUR?

Dinosaurs were not just ancient reptiles. Scientists have discovered this by comparing the bony skeletons of dinosaurs to reptiles, such as modern crocodiles and lizards. Most reptiles have a hip structure that makes their legs sprawl out on either side of their body.

So they can only lift their bellies a little way off the ground and must swing their bodies side to side to walk forward. But dinosaurs had a hip structure that put their legs directly below their hips for better body support. That let a dinosaur lift its body off the ground and easily walk or run straight ahead. Some dinosaurs could even stand and move on just their two hind legs.

crocodile

T. rex

Not all kinds of dinosaurs lived during the same time period. Check the timeline to see which of the featured dinosaurs was alive when.

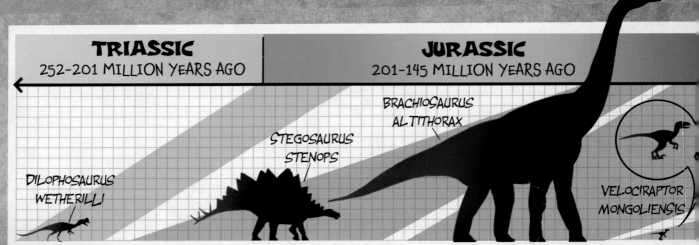

TRIASSIC
252–201 MILLION YEARS AGO

JURASSIC
201–145 MILLION YEARS AGO

DILOPHOSAURUS
WETHERILLI

STEGOSAURUS
STENOPS

BRACHIOSAURUS
ALTITHORAX

VELOCIRAPTOR
MONGOLIENSIS

WHY AREN'T THESE DINOSAURS STILL AROUND TODAY?

Scientists believe the Age of Dinosaurs ended around 66 million years ago.
There have been many theories over the years as to why this happened. Here are the two most popular with scientists studying dinosaurs today.

1. A giant meteorite fell from space. When it struck Earth, the meteorite kicked up so much dust that the sunlight was blocked, killing many kinds of plants. Without enough food, the plant-eating dinosaurs died. Then meat-eating dinosaurs died.

2. There were huge volcanic eruptions that lasted thousands of years. The gases given off were poisonous, and the volcanic ash in the air blocked off sunlight. That caused the same deadly chain of events: Plants died, followed by plant-eating dinosaurs, and then meat-eating dinosaurs.

Either of these could have happened. And, in fact, some scientists believe **both** did, bringing the Age of Dinosaurs to an end.

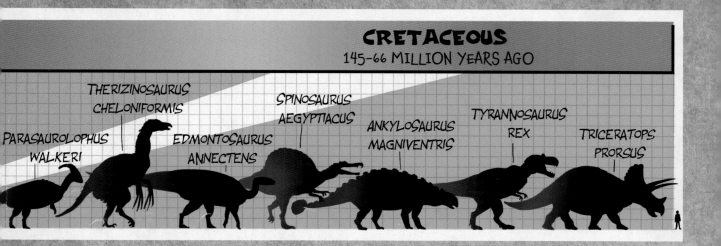

CRETACEOUS
145-66 MILLION YEARS AGO

PARASAUROLOPHUS WALKERI

THERIZINOSAURUS CHELONIFORMIS

EDMONTOSAURUS ANNECTENS

SPINOSAURUS AEGYPTIACUS

ANKYLOSAURUS MAGNIVENTRIS

TYRANNOSAURUS REX

TRICERATOPS PRORSUS

OTHER BOOKS IN THE SERIES

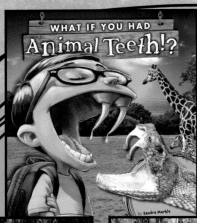

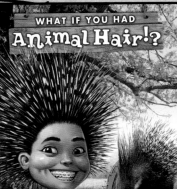

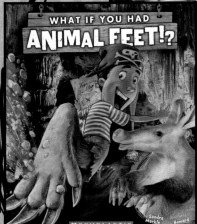

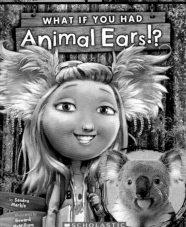

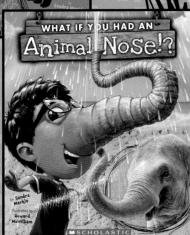

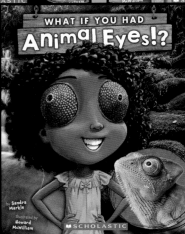

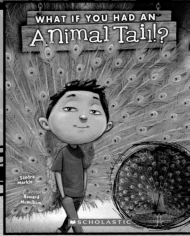